Growing Wings: A Story in Poems

Janet Akselrud

BookLeaf Publishing

Presentation by *BookLeaf Publishing*

Web: www.bookleafpub.com

E-mail: info@bookleafpub.com

ISBN: 9789357212779

First edition 2023

I appreciate being in a new place.

It shows that somehow I've changed,

enough to be where I didn't think I could be.

*This book is dedicated to everyone I've crossed
paths with*

who has helped me find my way.

ACKNOWLEDGEMENT

Thank you to all who proofread drafts of my poems and gave me opinions on the title and cover design. Thank you as well, for being excited about the story I could share.

PREFACE

Dear Reader,

I humbly welcome you to the first book I have ever published. It is my joy to share this moment with you, to share a piece of my heart and my memories with you.

Right before I chose to create this book, I spent a lot of time thinking logically. This made sense, given I was taking many math classes, but I noticed something didn't feel right. I had spent so much time on logic that I neglected the creative side of me, and my energy drained without being refilled.

As soon as I realized this, I took out my art supplies: paper, paint, markers, glue, and went wild. As Henry David Thoreau says "all good things are wild and free." Then I saw the words "poetry challenge" from the corner of my eye, and jumped at the opportunity to be a part of it (the result of this challengs is the book you are reading). It was a split second decision that I have been both nervous and excited about.

Writing new poems and editing old ones has been a reminder of the adventures I've been on, the feelings I've felt, and a reminder of how essential expression and creation are to my being. There is no reason to hold back. There is all the reason to have the courage to share.

I encourage you to do the same. Let magic and intuition guide you.

Sincerely from the author,
Janet

P.S. You can send me a message! A hello, a hi, your thoughts, a story that one of my poems reminded you of… my email is h.dashnarquitectures@gmail.com

P.P.S. Weew buco ucqy bjev ydtc omur iyju Jxum uriy juyi qcki ukce vcom ehar kjyj yiqb ieqj huqi khus xuij jxqj sedj qydi ejxu hset uive hoek jetu shof jYvo ekvy wkhu tekj jxyi cuii qwu iudt cuqd ucqy bmyj xjxu meht ifkc fayd icqa ujuq

Looking For Leprechauns

A rainbow landed at my door
Did it find what it was looking for?

A hand to be held by
eyes to ignite
skin to color
a heart with which to take flight

Someone different
at least in some sense
from those who don't understand
rainbows just want a friend.

We tend to think that rainbows
are outgoing and bold
but they're shy, they like to hide,
they run away,
because people chase them for gold

And what other choice do they have
when they're told by the world
that a leprechaun's home
is their job to expose?

They're friends with the leprechauns
Is that something you knew?
Why else would rainbows shine
in the bright mornings dew?

Why else would they sparkle
in the leaves of the trees?
And even exist
in a warm summer breeze?

So you see rainbows are loyal
to the friends that they have
but they don't have the words
to say no to the job

In turn, they pretend,
they send a sign then they run
it's a game that they play
which has lost all its fun

because they're tired of running
from those they can't trust
and want to spend time
with those who have colorful hearts

those who spend time in nature
and see magic untold
those who want to be friends
without looking for gold

There are humans like that
all over this Earth
but they go by a different name
"Leprechauns"
maybe you've heard.

In The Forest

I know a place that hides a secret
which might be useful to the world
but, I don't know how to describe it
so it's not in danger of being sold

I wouldn't want to share it
even if I could
or,
maybe I would

No, I wouldn't
because even artifacts of old
are more beautiful
than gold

I also know where magic comes from
and how to see it time to time
but I don't know how to describe it
though I don't want this power to be just mine

I know I see, I know I feel
Yet the words, they kind of disappear
because magic cannot be contained
it changes form,
it plays a game

So even if I tell you
the object I can see
it's not the object I am looking at
it's something deeper, something I feel

My heart I can't put into yours
but you can come along with me
to find a spark that lights your own
by seeing me watch what I see

Can You Hear My Silent Smile?

Can you hear my silent smile?

The one ignited by simple words…
"Bella, I love you"
sent my way sincerely,

the one whose roots break through the darkest
corner of my soul,

the one whose branches reach the light
and remind me
that the surface is connected to the depths,

the one whose fruit radiates in every emotional,
spiritual, and physical realm

I feel
held but not confined
warm but not burned
loved.

The People

It's quiet. They're gone. This doesn't feel right.

It's as if the blanket I just began to snuggle into
got pulled off my body on a cold winter day.

It's like a fresh river of warmth, love, and
acceptance,
suddenly ran dry.

The canyon built by it's waters
reveals an abyss

who's depths I must keep myself from getting
lost in.
But, it's okay.

I've seen this river before,
and been held by this blanket before,

I trust they will find me again,
or that I will find them.

Until then,
I sit at the edge of the abyss, feet in,
looking up,
waiting for rain.

The Night Love Struck Me...

What the F——- is life?

Oh my goodness.
I love him!
I guess it was love at first sight

and then we kept talking
I always wanted to sit next to him,
for him to be next to me

I wanted to stare into his eyes forever
I felt pulled in his direction.

When I looked at him
I would unknowingly smile

When we sat together in the dark
he kissed me on the cheek and held my hand
fireworks ran from my head to my heart.

I wanted to kiss him
but man,
I held myself back.

I can't be with him,
or is that just in my mind?

I don't know

What if the love was because
I was exhausted?
and he was on a few beers?

but
then again
the day we locked eyes,

*

he knew, I knew,

It was as clear
as a cloudless sky

What if it was something?
What if it was beautiful?

December 27th 2020

"I love too much and too many"

My mom responded,
"You will learn to love less as you get older."

"Is that a good thing?"

Resisting Gravity

What is this light I can see in your eyes when
you smile?
this spark, that pulls me closer to you?
I feel myself getting lost in your gaze, and I will
be the first to look away,
but only so as not to fall in love.

You feel it too,
gravity warping around us,
time holding its breath.
The strength of our intertwining energies gets
stronger the longer we stand.

Your certainty in your own essence radiates,
the knot in my stomach breaks apart,
warmth from the love I was hiding ripples out
from my heart.

All I want is to take a step forward,
give in to the riptide
to let my face gently rest upon yours.

I'm sorry I stepped away.

Could you tell I didn't want to?

Now I'm halfway around the world, still diving into the memory of the moment we shared. One day, together alone, I'll let go of reality, dive into your world.

Every End is The Start of a New Beginning

Every death of a galaxy is the birth of a new
one,
Every end of a day, the start of a new one,
and it's never really an end, never really a
beginning
but logic doesn't work to override feelings,
because again,
I'm leaving.

I've never really moved houses,
My so-called "home" has always stayed in one
place,
but I've moved my life back and forth between
countries

and at this point I'm tired of moving so much
of loving and leaving
a piece of my heart
in all of these places so that
I no longer feel whole
no matter where I am
no matter what part of the world
because a piece of my heart is always
somewhere else too

I'm tired,
but how do I stop?
and most importantly, where?

I can't stop anymore because it's already done
stopping won't bring me the places I've gone
and now every end is never just this one
it's the one before and the one before that and
the one before that

and people say "wow
she's been everywhere,
I want to travel just as much too."
but every time they say that, all I think is
:(

I get to learn and change in every new place
but I come back to people who expect me to still
act the same
and every goodbye is a little heartbreak,
yet most family and friends don't see I need tape

I haven't traveled enough to lose a sense of who
I am
but I have traveled enough to not know where to
fit in
not knowing where to call home
I've stopped even asking the question

because I have no clue where to begin to look
for an answer

but "where is home?"
is less important to know
then "when will love be?"

…

The first end was the hardest
because I really believed
each goodbye meant forever

that the people I felt love for,
I would see maybe never

The second time
I didn't cry as much,
for I tried very hard not to open my heart

The third end,
I cried even less
I just didn't engage so I'd have less to miss

But then I traveled again and again
and for longer periods of time,
soon my heart got tired of hiding,
it welcomed new love and allowed me to shine

I learned not to build walls,
to just let myself cry
not only for the past
but in the present when saying goodbye

It was the 17th time I said goodbye
that I accepted
this is my life

It isn't just something out of the ordinary,
it isn't a blue butterfly, or a four leaf clover,
it's an orange butterfly, a three leafed clover.

it's happened before and it'll happen again
if I leave what I love, it's not the end of love

Balance By Extremes

It smells exactly how a beach should,
of wet sand,
sunscreen,
and salt.

Outside the water, it's so hot
Inside the water, it's so cold

Standing half inside, half outside,
you are hot and cold.

But you swim in the cold ocean water,
come out to the hot summer air,
and you feel perfect!

Each deep breath in ignites content,
waves crash onto shore,
I watch and I listen,
to the sound

of not wanting anything more.

Plum Poem

I walked into the darkness
and found a lonely, purple plum
I knew it did not belong there
so I had to make it gone

I stomped on it with furry heels
I squished the parts I didn't smash
I made sure no piece was whole
like window glass after a crash

But I didn't want to spread it out
and leave a purple trail
so I slipped my feet out of the heels
and barefoot, walked away

There was nothing in the further darkness
nothing I could see
I couldn't see my hands
or any plum fruit tree

I sat down and stayed quite still
until my stomach rumbled
and that's when I realized
the plum could have been my supper

——------so I rolled back

and touched the place I smashed the plum
but, plum pudding I had not made
instead it was flat like dried purple paint

and the heels were flat too
as if I never wore them
they were all just pictures
on a floor that could hold them

but now nothing seemed broken
nothing had to be fixed
I guess same goes for anyone
even in the peak of their solar eclipse

Darkness isn't Dark

I want to take his hand and spin into his arms
I want to sway together underneath the stars
He taught me darkness isn't dark
and that the world can't fall apart
because it's already falling

I want to be in his arms
I want to dive into his eyes
I want to hold his hand
walk under the moonlight

But, I don't know
If he ever thinks of me
If what we had was gone in our very first week
If the words we said,
the silences we shared,
lost their power and depth,
dissipated.

I wonder
if he really meant,
that if I said yes,
theres no one he would ever
look at again?

I want to text him "hello"
ask how he's doing
but i'm scared to know
that he's moved on

even though at times I think I have

I want to take his hand and spin into his arms
I want to sway together underneath the stars
He taught me darkness isn't dark
and that the world can't fall apart
because it's already
falling

What If Everyone's A Pulsar?

"You only notice the light
when it's facing you…"

What if everyone's
a pulsar,
spewing light
after near death?

All the while spinning,
appearing,
to be there

and then gone.

Inconsistent,
even conditional.

But no.

I see now
the light is always there,
even when it's not shining
where I am.

** A Pulsar is a type of star

Stars Twinkle Overhead

a chorus of crickets
plays
beneath my feet

the end of summer air
surrounds
like a never ending
warm embrace

slow steps
unknowingly guide
toward one illuminated spot

A shadow of this figure of stone
silver and squiggly
an unnamed work of art

until I give it a name:
Monsieur Swan

I stand in her presence
drowsy,
open,
defenses relaxed

Am I alone?
I ask

no response

I don't know that you're real
you don't know
that I am

only I know
that i'm real

I, only, know
that i'm real

If only I, am, real
only then
I am alone

My eyes wander
to the depths of dark
beyond the one illuminated spot

three deer freeze in their tracks,
we make eye contact

I explore their gleaming stare
awaiting,
an answer

My hands begin to shake,
my mind still spiraling away

before my vision blurs
the trance breaks

I stop
my train of thought
I am alo… NO!

Create

Open a door
see what you haven't before
imagine a world
unimaginable

From one door to the next
each holds within
the unique possibility
to or not to exist

until

YOU turn the doorknob,
put paper to pen
then existence is certain
you hold it within

Growing Wings

I felt I escaped
the world of steps set in stone
when I looked at my feet
and they were neither concrete nor cold.
When I saw I could walk
just as well on the dirt,
I could steer, and take off,
even fly.

I was bound not
to Earth neither sky.

Above & Below

I wish fish could fly with birds
and birds could swim with fish.

Air
Water
Wings
Fins

Flying and swimming are different
parts of one mix.

What if surface was nothing
but a mirror of worlds?

Could the sky be the ocean?
And space be the soul?

I'd like it to be,
and that's why I wish
for fish to swim with birds
and birds to fly with fish.

Treasure Is In The Stillness

Nestled in the water's depth is stillness.
A fishing line taking the plunge,
forms the only ripple.
It's grasping for a glimpse of treasure,
settled on the bottom level,
while the fisherman awaits a signal.

What's All This About?

Why do poems have to
be
about something?

Why do "good" books
have to be analyzed,
dissected for their meaning?

How do we know the words we read,
"between the lines,"
were left there to be found,

and are not just our own truth
reflected
as someone else's sound?

Out, Up, & Away

People say "think outside the box," but I've
realized maybe everyone is overthinking. All
you need to "think outside the box" is to:

get out of your bed
and out of your room
look up from your phone
and away from your book

step out of your house
and out of the store
look up at the sky
and away from the floor

walk out of the barn
into which the cows keep on coming
though it's burning on fire
and the smoke is engulfing

forget about cities and countries,
time zones and street names,
about titles and homework,
computers and bored games

take one piece of chalk,
draw a square on the ground,
step in then step out,
puzzle pieces will be found.

Puzzle Pieces

I have many puzzle pieces
they show up at random times
Which puzzle do they belong to?
I can hope it's one of mine

How high will they be?
How tall? How wide?
How many puzzles will I complete
before the moon rises the tide?

I don't know
but there's no box
I make the rules
and choose the ones

that go together
until one day
something clicks.
and makes me say

"Eureka!"

Eureka!

Do you remember when I asked you about love?
about how it feels when it's unconditional?

I asked because I felt it from you
but I wasn't sure because it was so new

You took a breath and held my hand in yours
Your eyes met mine and you said "well now you
know"